CW00832186

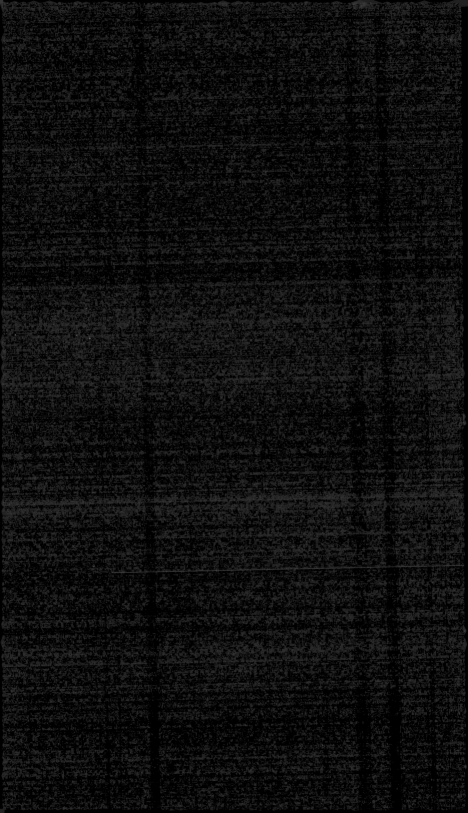

shadow dogs

natalie whittaker

ignit/**on**press

for Tom

First published in 2018
by **ignition**press
Oxford Brookes Poetry Centre
Oxford Brookes University
OX3 0BP

© Natalie Whittaker 2018

Cover Design: Flora Hands, Carline Creative

A CIP record for this book is available from the British Library

ISBN 978-1-9997412-7-3

Contents

96

A chicken box ricochets down the aisle: *Hot*
& Tasty - just the way you like it! Tonight,
the pigeon-shit town washes by, under a cold
and tasteless sky; this place where we've wasted
our lives like two spiders circling a sink.
And the plastic seats swing through the streets
and the STOP button shrieks at you to STOP,
but the silver trace of everyone's day has fogged
the top deck windows, and you dare to wipe
your name in the breath that's censed a hundred
rain-bedazzled hoods; knowing that the cost
of those letters in condensation – your
wet syllables ghosting sodium light –
is the use of all of those strangers' breaths.

Stag-girl

It starts with a spilled pint
spreading like a blush across my lap.

You flash a red napkin
from a stack on the bar; you dab,

dab, then catch my eye:
a glance like a chariot

ploughing the empty air between us.
You aim a sickle of a smile

as antlers sprout, bristling, from my scalp.
It's all in the look:

a taut bowstring; a quiver
that unleashes howling hounds, unbidden.

Moss

That winter I was under the influence
of moss. The first sign was a taste
for sour milk; I'd watch it cloud and spore

in tea, its spiral galaxy expanding.
Next, I decorated the flat with green doormats
and X-rays of smokers' bronchial tubes.

I imagined the countryside, where moss
would bloom over wells, stone bridges and troughs;
a place where I could let the moss

moss over me. Instead, I slept in the shower;
curled around the plughole in a damp bikini,
fingering clumps of pubic hair. I brewed soup

in old plant pots. Threaded spinach
between my teeth. Powdered my cheeks with mould.
I longed to be lichen, to breathe salt air

until the nightmares of limpets began;
their radulae rasping my flesh from rock
then leaving, returning to their home scars.

Not Again

When I came home that night you were raving
to the shipping forecast in the kitchen,
moving with the grace of a broken puppet
and wearing the hair of the dog; his brown fur.
I said *you bring me peace like an earthquake.*
You turned on the smashed-up tiles and said *watch*
what happens when one person screams at night
then screamed at the night. The whole city screamed
back; echoes smacking around cars and lamp posts.
Only the shaved dog stayed silent. I knew
in the morning the sparrows would drop eggshells
like our thoughts all snappish and empty,
and somewhere a fox was gargling acid
and fishponds reflected the obvious stars.

Boat Party

The Thames is electric and the evening drunken; the lighting rig spinning pink and green out onto the river; every highlight on the water like a fag butt briefly sparkling then trod on, every ashy constellation lost in others. Below decks, it's hip-hop vs RnB and I think hip-hop is winning, just. We pass under Hungerford Bridge and for a few seconds worry that people will gob on our heads and in our pints, but then, in the space above a paddle steamer moored on the Embankment, the Houses of Parliament put their hands in the air, raise gun fingers to the sky, and some guy gives the finger to the building in general and shouts *fuck those pricks!* and we all laugh and repeat *fuck those pricks!* but I'm sure everyone is thinking of a different, individualised prick or set of pricks. We chug on into a Sex on the Beach-coloured sunset, and the moon is raw like a spot of flesh under peeled sunburn, and inside the crowd hammers on the low gilt ceiling as a track drops, and later there'll be ringing in ears and later there'll be strobes like lightning.

The Ring-Necked Parakeets
of South East London

are screaming and green;
in their hundreds they lift

from fired-up trees
and flee over luminous joggers,

reined lurchers, a lake,
into a highlighter-pink sky,

as beyond park gates, rudeboys rev
their snarling engines.

And if night starts anywhere, it's here:
the earth leaching light from the sky

as the sun's dusty projector bulb dies.
We splash through dark that pools on paths

and run from the evening that roosts,
silencing the suburbs.

Stay

A dog's shadow crosses the park. Let loose
off its black lead it sniffs and is sole
eyewitness to empty booze bottles
tangled in nettles; the necromancy
and parliament of the previous evening
where we exercised our shadow dogs
on the slopes up to the smashed-glass hothouse,
fearing their size in the heartthrob dusk,
their stilt legs stretched and monstrous
as the sun sat obediently down.

The Honeymoon Suite, London Zoo

I like to be alone between the breeding tanks,
listening to the bubble generator's breathing
in a place where hosepipes dribble
puddles that smell of the ocean.

I move through the warmth of the live food room
where I incubate algae in flasks; living,
gurgling, green, ticking off each feed
– frozen Artemia, Mysis, live Artemia –
from a clipboard stained bloody with rust.

Everyone knows how they mate, how the males
give birth, but not how much practice the dance takes,
the pairs travelling up and down the tanks,
riding on currents; how darkness rushes
to extremities, painting their edges.

They don't know how I've held the short-snouted
hippocampus hippocampus outside in the air,
its prehensile tail clinging to my finger, strong
like a baby; how at night I dream

of floating, of weeds wrapped around my ankles,
krill crushed and stinking on my fingertips;
how I see fry born with two faces, born without mouths,
the mass of carcasses fished out with a net;
and their hearts, kept in the back of their heads.

Pebbles

Do you remember how we stumbled
down that tipsy pebble beach,
and cried out at the tilting night sky
that shook silver coins into the ocean,
a spilt glass of black wine. Or how
the constellation of a ship went by:
white-red-white. Or how, that night,
our tongues oiled with happiness, we shied
pebbles at the sea, but threw to miss.

I am a Morning Person

but only when that morning
brings two bluebottles droning
like tiny chainsaws to the shower
bouncing off black tiles
like electrocuted prunes

and only when that morning
commences with me whipping
one bluebottle to death
with a white towel then washing
its body down the drain

and continues with me leaving
the other fly alive
for just an hour and writing
I WANT A BABY onto
a single sheet of loo roll

I DON'T WANT A BABY
on another, then watching
from the doorway to know
which the doomed but living fly
lands on, and makes true.

To the Giant Ground Sloth
in the Natural History Museum

You surprised me, lurking in a gallery
of framed plesiosaurs and ichthyosaurs
– those fossils like fish bones on tinfoil –
but pleasantly; not like the stranger
in a stained tracksuit who flashed his cock
in an underpass when I was fourteen.
They've given you a tree to embrace.
It's branchless; you caress its smooth bark
between broad claws and stumpy legs
cast in plaster under Victorian arches.
Evolution reduced you; forced you
to climb trees you once stood eye-high to.
Evolution exhausted you. Your shadow
rests on bricks the shade of old urinals.

Five

I'm down the shed end of the garden
by a splintered sun-bleached fence
overturning the worlds of woodlice and snails

when I shift a house brick with one foot
and a frog – a shred of lime elastic –
springs at me. I stamp on it. And my mum sees.

It was a baby and you killed it.
That same year she takes me to the railings
of big school. A cage of screams.

Guy's Hospital, October 2015

In the waiting room a game show called *The Edge*
combines bowling skills with general knowledge.
Nobody watches or changes the channel.
I carry a chewed polystyrene cup

to the ward that's wired with orange poison.
There's a woman who looks worse than you,
wearing a cold cap that fuses *Tron*
with 50s swimwear fashion. Her husband

loiters. I think *please never let this happen*
– I give you water – *to me.* Your fingernails
are gone. Outside the window, sunlight streams
through The Shard and London Bridge Station.

The Corner Cafe

I'm sat outside *The Corner Cafe*, which I still pronounce *caff*, not *ca-fay*. A siren scatters pigeons and I have to keep shifting the table and my position at the table to keep my face in the sun. The sun is reading me over the shoulder of a tower block, like the one I didn't grow up in, but my dad did, and that I visited every Sunday for twelve years; where we'd go up in the steel lift and my nan would say *mind the corners girls, there's tiddles in the corners,* because men pissed in the corners. I've finished my panini, and it's not a toasted sandwich, it's a fucking *panini*. A van hesitates before taking a sunlit parking space, and I let the waitress take my plate. My first job was washing plates, which applies to most people, I know, but I'm the only person I know who was dropped off at Oxford in a Transit van. And when I was a baby in that flat, my nan would wash me in the sink and put me on the side to dry, like a plate. For a minute the traffic goes loud, like some cars all suddenly escaped from somewhere. And then my mum calls my phone, and I know that I have that voice, like a seagull circling a tip; and I'll always feel this little bit ugly and broken inside, like a washing machine left out on the street, but now I'm writing that down, I'm not reading *The Sun*, or eating my tea off a tray, and now I'm forcing a point, and I suppose what I'm trying to make myself say is something like *sometimes I don't know what to say.*

Bait

He loved to tell the story of the time he carefully spooned
a pint of maggots through the letterbox
of the *miserable cow* who lived three floors down.

I'd imagine them clagging the black bristles like eyelashes,
their sawdust-coated bodies, rainbow-dyed from the tackle shop,
crying onto her doormat. I'd wonder

how long it took for their scattered colours
to fill her flat, whether they got as far as her toothbrush,
her pillow, before she got back, and I hated

the idea of him doing that, and being my dad.
I sat half-impressed, half-terrified, hooked
in a room full of eyes that watched but did not blink.

Thoughts are Origami Birds

tied to the tree that branches from my scalp.
They snap from their strings in the lightest wind.

Sometimes I can hear a real bird singing,
lost beneath the papery flapping

of those folded mathematical birds
and the rasp of branches scraping the sky.

Question One

We spent Monday nights drinking in The Railway,
our team name tattooed through beer-soaked clue sheets.

When asked about you, I never knew the answer.
But there is that photo of us, laughing on that broken-glass

park bench in Barcelona: everyone else dressed for cold
while we're in sunglasses; winning for ten sparkling minutes.

Fenced

The smell of next door's dog shit slinks
through football-smashed fence panels,
stubborn as South London self-esteem; *no
one likes us, we don't care.* Their kids
don't care for privacy; trampolining
up against the back wall, sniggering
as I sunbathe. Our garden is stitched
with weeds and no, I realise, I don't care.
A few fences over, a man calls his daughter
with my name, and my sense of self slips
like Adidas bottoms on a leatherette settee.
Bluebottles thread the humming blades of grass,
and looking up through sunlight's needles
I wonder how much height of sky we own.

Winter Landscape with Skaters

An unwanted dog has been painted out;
whitewashed, like my memory of my dad saying
if you'd been a dog, I would have drowned you at birth.

The ghost dog is still there beneath the ice;
it barks up at the blades of skaters
as they cross the frozen surface of the lake.

Rope Trick

Tonight the circus burns orange. I grip
the bit between my teeth and step into empty air
as the crowd's breath balances, ready to tip
from gasp to scream at a slip of my tongue.

Brass notes well up from the ground;
a distant continent. My stomach is swollen
with sawdust, gravity and destruction.
I tread the music; stomping on sound.

In air, my element, the crowd roars my name.
I flick my arm like the baby elephant's trunk.
Drum roll. A downpour of applause.
I'm lowered, spinning, through the frame.

Blackheath

Running across the dark heath in bare feet,
missing broken glass through drunken luck
was like everything else between us:
the dare, the laugh, the risk, the knowing
that we were only one step from pain.
Pissing about at the end of summer's
hottest day. The sudden giant drops of rain.

Acknowledgements

Grateful acknowledgements to the following magazines, anthologies and competitions in which versions of some of these poems have appeared: *Brittle Star, Poetry News, Aesthetica Creative Writing Annual, #MeToo: A Women's Poetry Anthology, South Bank Poetry,* The Bradford on Avon Poetry Prize, Poetry on the Lake, The Virginia Warbey Poetry Prize and the Plough Poetry Prize.

'Thoughts are Origami Birds' is based on the painting *Paper Birds* by Steven Kenny.

The line 'if you'd been a dog they would have drowned you at birth' is from 'Knives Out' by Radiohead.

Special thanks to City Lit, The Poetry School, The Arvon Foundation and Ty Newydd creative writing centre; without these organisations many of the poems would not exist.

Thank you to Helen Mort for awarding 'Stay' second prize in the Oxford Brookes International Poetry Competition, and to everyone at **ignition**press.